Barbed Forest

Bill F. Ndi

Langaa Research & Publishing CIG
Mankon, Bamenda

Publisher:
Langaa RPCIG
Langaa Research & Publishing Common Initiative Group
P.O. Box 902 Mankon
Bamenda
North West Region
Cameroon
Langaagrp@gmail.com
www.langaa-rpcig.net

Distributed in and outside N. America by African Books Collective
orders@africanbookscollective.com
www.africanbookscollective.com

ISBN-10: 9956-764-77-9

ISBN-13: 978-9956-764-77-8

© Bill F. Ndi 2017

Table of Contents

Jungle Lions

With leaden mane they laze
In their craze
In the Sahara and its South
Hosting many a hungry mouth.
In numbers here and there
Heading prides, the unselected few in the fields where
The cob lions adore using as their playground,
And looking up to the elders to turn things around
Heads of prides pride themselves kings of the jungle
And all would a melody from their roar jingle
But they wish all waited a while
As they for all, would time kill and whirl.
By them, they are the strongmen of their territory
And for many cobs they are the object of genuine pity
For they define their territory by such delusional names
Reflecting one of their favorite games:
Translating Libreville,
Prisonville,
Freetown,
Prisontown
Where all subjects they keep down
And subjects with known tragic flaw
Obey and abide by the law
Forgetting where the law is lawless
Its heads and its forces enjoy obeisance less
To their pleasure or displeasure
And from the People streams the measure
To assure the jingo does not cloud their minds
For it only serves as blinds
Screening the sun from providing vitamins

And stealing taste from the desired sacraments.
The lions lazing behind the pennon blast
Their music and would on to power cling to the last
And by such prefixes affix their names
As they with zeal burn like flames
Burning and burning the joys of all
Until the nations' complete fall
As they their grounds stand
And subjects would they could understand
The unreason driving the head lions mad
Declaring their Excellencies; sad, indeed sad!

Change II

Poets love, adore and cherish change
The junky in the streets would he had some change
So is it for the punk
As well as with the drunk
These poor souls would never see its sunrise
And the poet calling for one pays the price
For any such call
Standing him above the head tall;
Yet, change the throne would die for
Change the holy ground would it had four
If poets and people in the streets
See it far from anything coins and sheets
The throne and the mitre would embrace it in their pocket
To wield might and shoot like a rocket.
Toeing political lines one dreamer dreamt of this
And in the streets, all identified as his
For with him, might would visit them thus
And help sweep away obsolescence and its boss
When from the enterprise hurtled in a chide
And with him people were dubbed mad Xerox bona fide.
Given the folks do the desire nurse and see the difference
No care should be ministered the word game reference
And would the first estate put reason to motion
And stop hugging status quo to brandish 'n wield emotion
And with our hearts the People would relish the drink of
                                             change
Were it to come from the streets, the valleys or the mountain
                                   range
Real change the dream
And all would it flows like a stream

Or drop down like some fruits
Off trees with melodious sounds streaming from conduits
Driving fruit flies insane
To leave the place free of pain.

The Lion and the Lamb

Sheep have every reason to bleat
Spotting wolves around their domain beat
Their feet at the foot of their fence
And how they wish a lion came to their defence!
But the problem seen for the sheep
Is that their forte would never be sleep
In the jungle
With the coarse jingle
From lions' roar echoing some remote past
Yet, it rives in our world and fast
With lions thinking their manes
The sun of the jungle and the plains
Having finished the rams and the ewes
They blow away their fuse
Now, with just one little lamb
In the whole plain left, the lions with drool flood the dam
Loosing sight of the journey no tongue
Would tell and oblivious of the orphan's recital of a song
For this to come transport him to the land of glory;
His dream place to join ancestors in the rank of history
And happy too for the lion would tell of the last lamb
And the lion without prey would raise an alarm
And this won't be heard in the jungle
Not even when it be the loudest jingle.

In Search of Known Voices

Reminiscing the sounds of yesteryears' drumbeats
And falling apart in bits
All the voices have been swept away
And by dementia pushed to the bay
And not having heard any they know
They call the world home to partake in a show
In which they solicited help to find those voices
And all help they could receive were noises
And with nothing left but a haze
And with only one option to gaze.

Yet, they called in doldrums
Not in want of plums
So, please, beat and beat them the drums
Till ye drive the sounds they yearn into their drums!

Scavengers

You, you, you, and you see them as filthy filth
No doubt they live off the filth
But these scavengers need be treated with love
Not because they're stronger than the dove.

You, you, you, and you may not see the reason
Yet, in this nation lions hang on trees for "treason".

And Vultures flap their wings and send through the air
Fragrances and freshness all would wear and bear;
And when from their thrones lions with joy
Accomplish their favorite ploy
Albeit sick and unfit to rule
In the game they fix the rule;
Slitting the throat of a prey
And it is then that vultures prey
Cleaning the gory scenes of our pavement,
Driving quest for things more useful to cnvironment;
Some big fat cats do too no doubt
With Blake's, my family totem, making me proud
But not in seeing them strife on the living,
Not even when for them this rhymes with surviving.

Mare Providers

Fascination and awe grace repugnance for a lion
Be him in or out of his dominion
His characteristic strength to kill,
And he dexterously does with a thrill
Sending home a chill down the spine of the sleeper
Frozen by thoughts of terror provider proper
Found in lion kings like Suharto,
Polpot, Paul Biya, Momo, Nguesso, Bongo, Sese-seko…
The one and only thing none will stand to look,
A thing to make a nation puke
For the king is a lion in rage
Wanting in and mimicking lions' courage
Desolately in the marshes
Where, for the praise, he searches.

Blood & Fire

My pen wept
And silently waited for the head of this nation
To be swept
And swept away by flood
From the nation,
Its tears and blood,
The blood he has spilled,
The blood my pen did bleed
In stead of the suffering in this nation,
Save the king's
Who misery brings
To deprive them of their own ration.

Like the eagle soaring high
My pen spat fire
To burn the king
In hopes of the day of reckoning
When power will return to the streets
Where it belongs and not on sheets
Altered at the king's guise
For this sleazy disguise.

Today, lamenting over my people's plight
News came to me my country tonight
Bathes in blood and is on fire
And by thoughts of extrication from the quagmire
Carried away, I sat up to do justice
To my people who've only borne injustice.
So, I have to burn at midnight
Its candle before going to bed tonight

And hoping it brightens the warriors' path
For laughs, smiles and jubilation as aftermath
Of a struggle for freedom
Which for years eluded the kingdom.

Ticket to Freedom

Bundled in the knowledge
Of lying free and still
And as stiff as steel
Six feet under with no hedge
And no worries of any toil
And turmoil
No attacks of profound melancholy
Provoked or unprovoked, all gone instantly
Make nothing worth this ticket
Not even a win by zillions of a wicket.
She frees all from all
She stills stiff all
In the cavern six feet under
Where all will be forever
In the castle one will never have to share
And there all shall freely fare.

Little Lambs with Backs to the Wall

I was having a good, good laugh in my dream
When suddenly I heard a scream
And interrupting my laugh, I stopped to look
And saw things have changed not by the book
For the scream actually came from a lion
Chased by lambs reminding him of his transgression;
I looked again and again to see.
Lambs really they were in their primacy,
Meek, weak but strong-willed to avoid the bleak
Terror that pushed them back to the wall of brick
To seeing themselves on the dinner tables
They pushed the lion to try vegetables
And in their own hands took control,
Control over their fate, making it their main role,
With backs to the wall fighting back
With valor most think they lack
And I would you see the strong lion squeak
Squirm and scream, scared to the peak.
It might have been a dream
A reality transcending its realm!

The Silent Witness: the Living Brook

For many many years the brook snaked through
Silently and witnessed the king kill at will too!
With his sharp edged sword in the jungle, he didn't know
The brook would one day put up her own show
And her best example would be none but him king
Who has terrorized and would all his glory sing.

Each time the lion savoured his kill
Up stream he went not up hill
To wash blood off his mane & down his meal
This was life for him and the only thing real
He washed innocent blood in the brook
And one fine morning she her head shook.

The blood of the innocent in her left each time
Gave her life and strength to fight the crime
That left her heart as sore as mine
And she and I dreamt of the day things will be fine
For me to stand by her with my heart pounding
For, the long awaited treasure and pleasure, finding.

She waited
I waited
She took the like of an awe inspiring snake
Ready for a kill and would the lion take
And on her table feast
On the terror breeding beast

In quest of ending the gore
The king has made his lore,

We came face-to-face with the span of traditions
And took to ushering to oblivion, the lion's
So did we put the death bearer to rest in peace
Without a trace to warrant any feast for fleas

By the brook with no hook
But a smile I stood to look
And silently witnessed her accomplishing her feat
And silently snaking her way to the ocean meet
To let fall the king's bones
For the ocean to dust crush with his hones.

The Grass and the Beasts of this Earth

Carry their morning
Dew without pain
And quietly sapping
The ground without strain

The soothing green
Grasses in the plain
Must face the beasts' disdain,
For the beasts of this earth as seen

Over the strength impaired
Must have their triumph declared
And at top of voices sing
And treat all others worth nothing

In the fields where they stump
Beating the dew as they would the scum
Yet, the grass roots keep sapping
Like a grassroots' poet tapping

Inspiration from around
With his ears to the ground
Striving to see them survive
Even when they're set on fire live

They their ashes
Like phoenix's crushes
All hopes of never
Seeing them flourish ever

And the beasts must in her dwell
Whether or not they fare well
Living one with another
Always drawn together

Yet, one must dance their triumph
And the other would fight for triumph
In this world of inequity
With grass and poet dreaming of equality

Dialogue with Granny

Granny sat there with her pair of glasses
And pointed out the existence of only two classes
And I wished there weren't many more
For my chumps and I at school anymore…

"I mean in life," She insisted
"Those who in life labour,
Those graced at birth with favour,"
She contended.

"Two classes of people
And not those for a pupil."
Prompting me to look past the field
Where I sighted a beast of burden with no shield

Beside, I saw haunting armed claws ready to savour,
The poor helpless sheep as a guise for favour,
In ambush laying. Granny couldn't be anymore right
Everything viewed under this light

For, in her prolonged sightlessness
Her journey into righteousness
She continued and spotted the misdeeds
Of the corrupt coming out of their sheaths.

Nothing from Money

I see the eyes of the world on money
And many would like to taste honey

Then they embrace the first and head for hell
Even with the best of intentions armed well,

With no thought of anguish in the corner, a painful
One which money in a mansion full

Never will rid
And never will from the machine remove the grit

And for its part honey won't sweeten
For it's been blackened like a raven,

Desiring and pursuing money has always been
And not all in pursuit have money seen

Yet, it does still enchants their dreams
Until disenchantment flashes his beams

Then do things heat up
Where none thought of a hiccup

And reality knocks hard
Melting hopes and aspiration as lard

For them to sit up and think with more,
Their life and dreams wouldn't be such a bore

Yet, all see nothing from it comes
When all aspire something from it calms

That haunting anguish
Which only at death does humans relinquish;

Which served to distinguish the greedy
From them that embraced honesty

The thirst for money will never end
And will only a good anguish blend

For money was and is neither the alpha
Nor the omega from which it is far.

Midway Journey

We live with nature
We live in and by nature
Yet, from her we learn not
And by her example we live not

When in our journey we've hit midday
We needn't tarry, we needn't stay
For Donne's good busy old fool
Only knows when, where and how to sit on his stool

We fear the return journey
For the vacuum birthed on parting, a thorny
Path made the return so uncertain
Diminishing our wish for an outcome so certain

When even for good old Donne he shall die
We shan't be ready to fly
For a circle we're destined to complete
And not whirl time in life to compete

Nature Talks to a Lamb

Do not sleep meek little lamb
For you've got enemies in this land
Stray not farther afield
Stay in sight and your future build
Away from him that sees himself the ruler
Though not as straight as a ruler
And will not delight in you staying alert
For him to his might assert;
So, going to sleep, copy the fish
With your eyes open and be not the dish
For dinner for this prowler and entourage
Let your sleeplessness leave them in outrage
Your weakness from sleep comes
Sleeplessness your strength alarms,
Daunts and haunts them to seeing you silly
When with grace you graze prudently
To make the green of our fields greener
With rulers' fervour making the nation poorer.

Our Case

Kill our earthly stars.
What will you do to the heavenly ones?
To protect yourself, grease the soldiers' beard.
What shall you do when at your door death knocks?
Bring us the Opposition in a coffin.
But will you let us freely mourn?
You kill our poets.
Do you believe we will bury their writings?
Bury yourself amidst a zillion soldiers.
Haven't you learned from Chinese History?
Like you, in China one did this.
Did he not rot underground?
You sum your world with Law and Order.
Why let lawlessness and disorderliness reign?
You are god to those who buy your favors.
Who or what are you to those you deprive of sunlight?
Every night, you go to sleep on a king size bed.
Why not make your heart the size of your bed?
You ruin the nation to live in a mansion.
What space in it or our minds do you occupy?
You've dominated the nation tyrannically.
Shall you ever be the tyrant that kills death?
We thought to rule was to serve.
Why must a tyrant like you be served?
Now, to yourself, you've gathered the nation's wealth?
Won't you give us the right to determine the future of our
misery?
You push your tyranny, your greed and grip on power to the last
Won't you still be proven wrong from beginning and end?
You may never stand in front of any court to plead guilty.

But which other criminal supersedes you?
With your sentence as long as life,
Shall you in your dead bed rule over us?
You may never see this as a case.
But, here, are we not free to rest our case?

Before You Hang Me

Hate or oppress me
Hang or shoot me
Burn or bury me…!

But before this twist
Let me clench my fist
Let me provide a gist:

Let me sing
To the men and their king
A song that like bee sting

Awakes them to the load
Carried by us with a moral code
Reduced like some toad

Cast with a spell
Shut in a well
With no story to tell.

Hearing my song
They shall see what's wrong;
Take the orders then for me to be wrung.

Shooting, hanging, wringing solve not the problem
But attracts a boo for an anthem
Leaving blood, fire and grief as their emblem.

As of stone they have made their hearts
None will ever to them doff their hats

But all will confirm they replicate rats.

Then and only then
Smolder me, not my pen
With flames before I count ten.

Peacefully, I shall die
Heartily, my spirit will fly
Disgracefully, will the king comply.

I shall be death but not gone.
The People shall have, with the king, done
For prising from them their dawn.

Go Tell the King!

I don't mind him twisting reality
But assure him that won't sit in my cup of tea
If he wants to see
Me like a bee
Dance,
Of him I'd request no lance
Nor water canons or gold;
Our stolen treasure he's sold
But truth and untwisted reality
Solid foundation on which stands honesty.

Pol & Paul

Pol like Paul 'twixt believers and Christ
Stands 'twixt honest citizens and rights
Here, the Mungo 'twixt west and east frights

Conjure. Unlike them the Mungo Brings sand
With which we might someday erect a stand
On which we might unity brand

In hope of avoiding adversity
Where Pol would strangle liberty
As the earthly proclaimed deity.

God? He is far from
And evil does him adorn
And conscienceless has he the nation torn

Unwilling to make a turn around
Like Paul who after biting the ground
Was only after three days found

But, Pol would conscience by force
Comes, and happily would savour some human loss
Styling all the world's humane concern a fuss

Unlike Paul, Pol went to a seminary
To be schooled in the art of emissary
And far from Paul, Pol came out champion adversary.

The truth, he would none proclaimed
But all his lies, he would all acclaimed

Failure for which the nation is maimed

With Pol pushing her to a standstill
Killing to remain in power still
And plunging her into the abysm further still

If for all these, Paul was canonized saint
Then it is a story to make a nation faint
And call artists to the saint repaint.

Reparation Panic

The suits of wool they wear
The wool grew on sheep nourished by a forebear
None remembers and much less the grass it ate
And much less the blood that fate,
No! Man spilled to water the grass
That bloomed bright and shiny as glass
In the haven of multiculturalism
Where with utter awe and pessimism
The coalition mustered its might
To put up the biggest fight
Not to spare the Rudd and hear sorry
And in a gimmick, millions of light years
Embroiling and forgetting for years and years
They like frightened dogs
Their tails rapped forming a click of power hogs
And behind one queued and he down the abysm
And made his religion howardism
Today, we would they spare the Rudd
For us to hear sorry and not bear their rod
The like of our forebears whose blood this land painted
ULURU RED

Message Bearer to the Monster

Old bottle old beer
We are still and young
And won't cup your beer
Poisonously strong

Crime, your song in rhyme
With which you make merry
That we at our prime
Won't embrace from you pixie

Murder, your act for might
Does your ignominy crown
And we will fight
Till you are down

Police brutality, your shield
Sends reports of many a killing
And against it we stand in the field
Till the harm stops breathing.

Crushing our rights, your daily chore
Supper power support, you've got?
Listen, we are resistant to the core
And will never stoop to be treated like a sot

Your daily delight? A bottle of whisky!
My mind! You won the game?
We identify your voice, husky
And only you will shoulder the blame

Blood spills on our streets, your shame
Flood our towns and make us weep
Yet, with arrogance you sing fame
That is a cheap sweep.

New grave, new baby!
The nation is reborn!
Uplifting hearts happy!
With the monster gone!

Gainsay no true say
That's tribute to the resistance
For having with a thread woven this day
On which we downed the monster with brilliance!

Our Welfare

With such demeanor
Like a minor
The degree of liquor
In him sends languor

People stretched thin
Abandoned with nothin'
Cast an eye in a tin
To find somethin'

Not finding any
From the drunk they request money
But are sent a levy
Grandiosely done without privity

Gift from the government
Masquerading the torment
These power hungry lords foment
And won't want any to comment

The Sao

They were my forebears and must not be forgotten
Even if to the mortals they are rotten
Not in nature, but in their grave
For soldiers they're and of the stock of the brave
With voices to rend my fellow man
Hay wild. Now, found and dubbed desert man
Telling of the might that once was
Better than what in that cradle is seen as worse,
No, the worst. Life with its twists and turns
Surges forward and nothing ever returns
Like mine who were the Sao
And lived far from Sao Paolo
But could cough and fall down a tree
Over there to liberate without a fee
And real they were and not the giants
In tales about monsters and brigands
Who robbed in the days of yore
And at the helm today endorse gore
Or silently sap bodily juice
Like Hitler the Jews
In that very chapter
In which his head brewed the snifter.

Not Yet Burial Time

We had a link
To us she gave no drink
But eased our dialogue
Long replaced not even by monologue;
In short, her role the imp did abridge
Though she served as a bridge
Today,
Mute with no say
No dialogue
No monologue
Death silence
And no penitence
From the scalawag
Who his doglike tail does wag
Caring not if the nation is thirsty
And has so done for years close to thirty
And now we question for how long?
As we now need to stand up strong
And flex our muscles
To defy his muzzles.

The dumb and deaf we know
Let not speech flow
But would not divorce their nature
For an eerie present or future;
We shouldn't trade ours neither
But strive to have it better
Knocking off that which our way does bar
Be them the heads or not, take them to the bar
And get them drunk with justice

Against all their deeds that flirted with prejudice.

Till then it won't be burial time
Not until we've swept the crime
And the criminals away
With their dreams to sway
Us to rush Our Bridge to its grave
A thing for which all our lives we slave.
We must now let them know
The people and only the people run the show
And must not chant with them burial time
Before the people are with the time in chime.

Life Givers

Whenever a lion pounces on its prey
Death is what all foresee for the poor prey
Poor thing!
 Poor, poor thing!
And even from the dour Moor
Tears would pour!
As all would cry
Forgetting the exit in death lie.
Death, the platitude
Needs no acceptance with lassitude
Which needs be shown to the stalemate
Flown up to the heavens by the reprobate
Soul mate of ingratitude
Very low in attitude
Clinging on to an earthly seat
With only death to give a treat
When on him and like a lion it pounces
Showing how life bounces
Bouncing back to the living
With this imposed paradise killing
The gem of life in man
So, death we need not its end demand
For death gives life
The like of birth starting life;
A thought not new
Yet, must be stated anew
To prevent it from dying
In the minds of the living.

Of stagnation and progress

The essence of any true poet is not in the flesh
Though in his flesh are rhythm and rhyme fresh
Take him for a game, hunt him,
Shoot, skin and roast him
His star will shoot
To guide all those on foot
Projecting
The everlasting
Poets' substance, the light
Poets would for all shine bright
Even in their bleak and somber moments
They delight at feast seeing all with refreshments

The knave of this happy end
Darkness would the poet bend
And would people see not where they step their foot
For the substance in darkness is all about food
The poet and his light on its way
Kills and stows its happiness far away

In the melody rhyming
And with rhythm overpowering.
Of progress born is the light
And of stagnation ignited is the fight
With darkness wishing the poet's death
And the poet in its depth

Exposing the upheavals on the path
To progress and calling unto himself the wrath
Of angry darkness desiring the poet dead on the spot

For the world to see how he's got his lesson hot;
Not knowing the poet fears not the burn of fire
Nor the stab of a dagger and much less shocks from electric
wire

With all of this the poet is still and still wears his smile
And even knowing he is to live only a short, short while.

Still in adversity facing him
And singing when facing those
looking up to him
In the fight
To get rid of the blight
Tying people on the spot
When they need to trot.

Boxed in a Farm

Forlorn in the field, at one end gazing at the ratoon
The poor little boy had seen, only in his mind, a cartoon.

His seedlings fresh from the nursery in hand
Up he looked at the sun declining west
And reflected on what he thought best
When from his curvature all day he did stand

In himself, the poor little planter
A poet saw, not a potter
As thoughts ran through his head
With the world laughing at him instead

For in the clayey mud he stood
Of which only a pot could turn out good
And with his rattle head ghettoized in a box
Never will he embrace the brains of a fox.

Yet, there hopefully, his rice
He planted and for the next sunrise
Waited. His seeds spread in a kind of order
And he the force of order

Adorning a poetic license
With words here and there to make sense
Just where all see none in the mix
Of clay and that which little fingers transfix

Through her.
In a poem, look not far!
For the poem is its fertilizer
The boy's ratoon and transplants' fertilizer

Need
For feed
As his proem
His liking lit for a Poem.

And that evening greeted the first sketch from his mind
And all the oppression waived, he ne'er was blind!
And he sees, draws and hears the beautiful sunset
And listens to the music from his mind's trumpet.

In poetry, the poor little planter himself found
And cheerful he homeward bound
Freed from the farm box
And away from the predator fox!

Hangman

Priest: Remember this is a Confession!
          Profession?
Hangman: Hangman!
Priest: What man?
Hangman: Hangman, a profession so undesirable
          Drives wonder in me if History is reproachable
          For lauding those of Charles I and Louis XVI
          Making contributions to the page newly written
          In the History of Europe
          And indeed, using no rope
          To drag the old order out
          Introducing one, new and stout;
          And my wonder brings home the miserable
          And make of the sweeping change desirable
          Through a dialogue spurred by a street man
          With no need for a hangman.
Priest: Cleansed you are of all the hanging
Hangman: Hope my wages for this sin is not dying.
Priest: Eternal life is yours!
          Well, shouldered you your cross!

Bitter Pills

When thoughts and acts are by smoke
Darkened, there is no room for a joke!
N.M. swallowed the bitter pill
N.W. firm and strong with will
And on the ground
Now sees the ground
On which to understand
How N.M. could on his feet stand
And chose to go on all four
For his heart with sore
Plagued from quarters
Imagined far from quarters

Dixeption

Each time I listen to Nature
I hear voices so mature
And looking around, I see an alliance

Nature urges is a mesalliance
I call an attempt to calm my agitated soul
And calm, Nature, I let its course follow.

The Tyrant reigns supreme…
In his delusional scheme
Thinking, over his subjects, dominion

He has, when in death's opinion
He's just another knave
Thinking flirting the best way to behave.

The Tyrant may please himself
And when death shows itself
Might attempt distracting for doing its work

Death shall heed not and mock
The camaraderie tyrants did with him contract
And failed to spell out their aversion for the tract

Now, death at their door, they must go down
Were it in the morning, no waiting for sundown
The time is the time

Even when at the prime
Of life itself, they must go with woe

Having attracted many a foe

Peace with no restrain
Must reign;
A severe blow

Dealing to all tyrants here below
Crushing and undermining Nature and Man
Which all should reprimand.

Many a Heartless Ruler

Callous rulers are not few
Heating up the nation like fire
And folks express a need so dire
For a mouth piece to come spew

The rage and frustration
Rulers often ignore
Which the nation's heart gnaw
For the cause of liberation

Callous rulers crop with this excuse
Serving freedom to the people
And against them stand my spectacle
For the people's freedom slain by abuse

The Flash of Beauty

From the horizon your beauty
Did flash
Hardly
Did one think of a backlash

What a beauty, flashing!
What a beauty lashing and slashing!
The price for drinking you with the eyes
As ice solid will never melt like ice;

You, godly apple,
Juicy and appetising
To all eyes and making them wrestle
Thinking their dreams they were realising

But your flash
Did and does blind
To the reality that a lash or slash
From you will all grind.

The Child Downstairs

Down south I lived downstairs
And Gee! I dreamt of life upstairs
It was a dream!
Only experience could tell what it did mean

In a rush, seeking safety like a meerkat
I docked myself under my hat
And headed straight up North
Attracted by the lights like a moth

Up North I lived upstairs
Up North my everything was life downstairs
And though not of misery void,
Could not be painted a tasteless tabloid

That dream I had
That dream I told dad
And with a pat he my roots
Did show me my life of shoots

Before embracing my dream beauty
Ne'er had I seen a sight so dreary;
Benumbing with frost biting cold
Stealing from the sun's glow its gold

And the step I made forward
Revealed two steps backward
The embrace, the dread, the numbness, the frost bite
And I would never any mind divide

With head now to the East
With the sunrise I feast
And would you only a glance steal West
Where the twilights my sun take to rest.

Weak Strength!

Hide not insecurities
Behind firmness
That strength might weakness
Be, leading to casualties.

Be soft with him or her that does love you
And blessings never few will be
And dance you will as a happy bee
And perchance clamped, come will love to your rescue.

The Infidel Spouse

You go to church
I do not as much
But our thoughts?
One from droughts
Suffer
Proper!

Money,
    Money,
        Money!
Dream,
      Dream,
          Dream!
Will smile bring
Will fame bring
Will bring joy
Will give the children toy!
That's the groom to espouse
You voraciously browse
Crumbling under its weight
Smile, fame, joy and toy still wait
For hate, heartlessness, arrogance
And insolence unveil their fragrance

With my back against your dream
Savouring life by the stream
And aspiring no longer after her
But death to behind leave her
Seeing unfaithful will she still be
And even to money!

Honey!
    Honey!
        Honey!
Taste!
    Taste!
        Taste!
Bring sweetness
Kill bitterness
With such hearty drops,
But once past the taste buds…?
Dream or money,
Taste or honey,
Arrogance or sweetness,
Joy or bitterness,
Usher to a desert
Devoid of dessert…!

All Apostles?

What has a woman before marriage?
The size of a wasp!
What does she become after marriage?
A giant size WASP!

Did the French not say so?
Is there any who is a wasp?
Does any sting more than the giant size WASP
Killing the Red in the field where there's a knee grow?

Seeing the frail and feeble
Thrown into the wild for standing firm
For all they had was belief and no firm
And seeing not a sting feasible

Then an open arm they gave
And below the belt a blow did receive
Before opening the eyes to no reprieve
That not even the reservations its way did pave

Woman, woman,
Lady, Lady,
Liberty, Liberty
Why do this to Man?

Be him Indian or African, red, yellow, blue, black or white
Be him Buddhist, Christian, Hindu, Muslim, animist or
                                                    agnostic
Don't you see in the various creeds something apostolic?
Woman, why not aside set your spite?

Of Thugs and Witches

Make no mistake
For mankind's sake
Were one to pass on by the beach
Attribute not that to a witch

Who the best of the craft might possess
For when her turn comes, death'll take no recess
In bringing back to her, her inequities
Fuelling the flames to these penalties

And having tarried around a while,
None would go another mile
For the turn has come
To seek understanding and calm

True, thugs are in our Houses
Let not this blindfold realities
For, when to witches associated is every death,
Under the weather is imagination's health

Our thugs do slit!
Is this enough tilt
To buy them responsible
For every death possible ?

We can't ignore in the shadow
They put up real horror show
Far from the Rocky & behind the weather
Hiding to give the masses a chilling jitter

For these, they should give accounts
And reasons for their swollen accounts
And Why for their misdeeds questions crop,
And they hurriedly into the grave the questioner drop.

The thugs are but few
And would always jump the queue.
To them we must always stand
Till we can to all of them justice brand

Purging our Houses of the plague
That has our nations and lives put at stake
Not until then, the experience will always be bitter
And once done, all will experience something better

Stand up!
Stand up!
Push out the thugs!
Push out the thugs!

And make no mistake
For mankind's sake
Were a thug to be given a dishonourable discharge
By those he enslaved, let 'm have 'n explosive discharge

To match his thoughts of being bold
Let him face the real freezing cold
In which he relished many to perish
Using that as a proper power polish.

Thou shalt not kill
But as for thugs, thou can still

Most especially those hiding in the House
Not being that reflected in them, a prison mouse

Take them to the bars
Send them behind bars
Leave them there to rethink
With just some drink.

Senile Old Lion

I'll hang to see this lion
Its mane shake with no option
Wondering the maze in which caught he is
After his fill drinking from his

Cup with measures of wickedness fill'd
To finding himself with no prey in the field;
In the vast fields with grass richly covered
Only to be by the bleating lamb covet

When the king has tyrannized and all exterminated
And is with none left to be subjugated
And is wanting in storage for his might
All have rejected to make their plight

I'd laugh to see him yawn
And yawn at dawn
After the plain ridding of its fauna
And priding himself the examiner

A sight to see none he would
Not even with him venturing in the wood
Like a disoriented old lunatic
Dreaming he was once charismatic

Senile old lion
Lost is the dominion
To the flock of innocence and benevolence
You burnt with flames of malevolence.

The Two Majesties

With their golden gold mane
The sun and these lions dominion share
Breeding the quest, which of them be fair?
Lions oversee the earthly plain

And by the barbed forest they lie
And do demise minister
While rules D vitamin giver,
High, high in the sky

And when the day's end draws nigh
He, sitting up there high,
Majestically his throne
Reclines and sinks like a drone

While their majesties here on earth below
Drive their subjects to bellow
Then tyrannically head off to the forest
To wedge a war against sleep for rest

And I would the subjects forage
For voices and bellow with rage
Till lions step not out of the forest
For choosing to sell subjects' nest.

Reneging the manner of worshiping
Would humans to the sun sing
For his generous supply
That gladdens hearts from high up in the sky.

The New Saul

My baby ears savoured with pleasure
The Bible story of Paul who did treasure
Killing when he was Saul
The like of the crowned soul
In my part of the jungle
Who his way does bungle
To hugging that knight of evil
And chopping our fabric like a weevil.
And touched was that knight
By the light
In the broad light of day
And in darkness he did stay
A night times three
Then was set free.
In the light, our crowned Paul
Did start but was dull
And by this, rushed into darkness
Where he did to greed and heartlessness
Take
And like cake
Did enjoy them
And that with no problem…?
Remembering how he did come to the head
I recall all sat under a baobab tree shed
And from above parachuted by Redman
Came our headman
Like the book they used to promote gore
That since became, here, the lore!
Redman, Redman as a guise thou didst unseat a king
And with this one to justice thou won't bring

And I quest why?
And wonder where the truth does lie!
When he worse has done to his kind
As thou to thine did, though they're kind;
Doth thou on these grounds do embrace him?
Or art thou afraid of the fat he'll leave thee slim?
If thou art the light in defence of the defenceless
Here thou hast a case of helplessness
To defend and set crowned Saul on the path
Saul treaded on here on earth to avoid a second wrath.
Saul to Paul I love
This Paul with Saul hand in glove
I deplore
And do, the world to unseat him, implore.

Weeping & Wailing

Cry not my poor child!
Cry not poor, poor child!
So near can I hear you cry
Loud but for others a far, far cry
Though you wail, wail, wail,
Wailing out your travail
And with none budging, I ask why,
Why, why, why;
When for a sob
Those with their backs to your cry won't snob?

Cry not my poor child!
Cry not poor, poor child!
But tell those who snob
Your cry, you need not fill a tub
For your pain to stick out
When your cry supersedes loud
And if they budge not, ask not why
Why not ask why
For with the devil they now sup
And in darkness too; for with light you're up?

Dry your tears my poor child!
Dry your tears poor, poor child!
Your light in this darkness leads you
And to the right and righteous path too
For with age the tears will your maturity
Fertilize and wash her to purity
Forget not the tears, for you did cry
Forget not you did cry

And let none for thy sake this do
For it deals them a blow like to birds the flu.

Under the Baobab Tree

The old man I met
Under the tree sitting, nothing said
But from the depths of his guts
Did laugh to echo him nuts

Yet, the wrinkles on his face
Tells not of life with a mace;
Having seen and felt every pinch
Of life with trendy lynch doomed every inch

Of the way, my good old man,
This good old man
With his beards
His knees caressing needs no threads

To stitch a life torn and discarded
By wielders so much guarded.
Under the tree
As much as any would see

Now, by himself
And in sight, not a shelf
But a black pool of experience
Into which thrown, he taps his reference

To shape the world he so thought
Would have wrought
Glory, fame and friendship
And not in the drain them tip

And now contemplating this leafless giant tree
He envisions far from age free
But emotion free, yet so faithful a portrait
Of an emotion filled life in the strait

Within the Baobab tree so leafless
And never lifeless
Wherein dwells the Spirit of settlement
Sheltering anything disagreement.

The Drover of Apostasy
(Apostate of Equality and Social Justice)

Go not to the mountain top
And let not the mountain be that to stop
This music tune
That will all apostate have out of tune
Out of tune with their moral
And social
Injustice
Put and end that bliss
In which dwells the cadaver
Of our equality & social justice by the drover
And his apostles interred
Hoping our desire for them deterred
Forgetting in the herd sheep call nation
From the grip of the lion,
The more the poor little lamb does bleat
The more ewes heartily breeding greet
And do their Desire express
Not to the lion impress
But to tell him the lamb is the most to take
For in him is an ablution for their sake.

Of Lies and Ties

On the other side of the fence sitting
And on this other side of the fence eavesdropping
The bombshells of blasphemy and lies
To the world coloured crashed on the ties
And lauded the hell of a good person
And the lamb across the fence for this sin
Did pray and did the lord implore
To pity them that do lies colour
Be this to the lamb done!
Be this to the lion done!
Or again to the self for a gain
Which for other's life is the bane,
Loathed and lonesome
And won't even for the handsome
Go to meet the maker
And would rather the herd's life bleaker
On the other side of the fence sitting
And with a mask concealing killing
Like a wolf in our wool clothed
And ignoring that shall be spotted.

Give Them Back!

Peacefully we in darkness slept
With their torch to pierce our eyes they crept,
In they crept with guise of bringing light;
Up, we quest if darkness was a plight
When we would we photophobia espoused
To sooth the soul calm and sound with sleep roused.

Give them, give them back,
Give them back their light!
Give us, give us back,
Give us back our night!

That munificence misplaced
Equates one to be replaced
For we need not of our sleep
Make a baby sheep;
For our protection most she needs
And not their light of horror deeds

So, give them, give them back,
Give them back their light!
And give us, give us back,
Give us back our night!

Our night with its silent music
Caresses the soul of a mystic
Like a bird in broad daylight
From branch to branch in delight
Perching to sing a song
Against the many years of wrong

Give them, give them back,
Give them back their light!
Give us, give us back,
Give us back our night!

Their light with its cutting edge
Slaughters resting knowledge
Like soldiers at war with their sword
Heeding not Peace, the word
Slitting throats in gory fight
To export their torturous light.

So, give them, give them back,
Give them back their light!
Give us, give us back,
Give us back our night!

Lady Z

Lady Z, Sing, sing,
Sing and sing

Bowing down to your ladyship,
In Love, of none I dreamt but friendship

Believing: "no poet quakes!

Under the mass of adversity,
He embraces with sagacity."

Our story was this simple
And I won't add it a dimple

Yet, you multiplied your woes
And sent me many, many foes!

My thirst
Does quest:

What of Ogden, the poet
Who of everybody a poet

Makes?

Or did her ladyship for moneys
Trade the universal man of justice?

This I thought her ladyship above
Most especially thinking we were in love

And still a poet, I won't fake
My commitment, your blows I did take!

No more ripple
I won't dribble!

Only wonder if you can swear
As I do of our love its garment wear!

Still will bow to your ladyship
And still of none dream but companionship

Sing, sing, sing to us a song
And asleep we won't see you wrong!

Platter of Abuse

Counting beads,
Stalling breeds

Serves not just

My cute,
Cute

Suit on libel
On each face
Without pace
Leaving a wrinkle

On a suit
That's my fruit,

To dribble
Like ripple
Sounding
Echoing
Tornadoes with Abuse
On a platter for their use
With icy cold
Callous gold

To be honoured
And honoured

And to face charges
And charges

But from human eyes slays trust

T' hailing them great men!
For 'razing the stamen!

Yet, would the platter bury
Or explode with fury

For this act so devilish
To a nation they by day ravish

Against this abuse
Justice should run in for use!

Earthly Wealth, Pious Dearth

Their earthly wealth
Of pious dearth
Draws to their retina
To the throne of Regina
Not the squalor
Taken for the nation's parlour
And we hail our kings here on earth
Who on their stools nod with mirth!
But let's remember
Ours we must recover!

For the oculist may sight
Restore to the wight
We as mite see
Charging a fee
And who in the wrong
Claims our rights wrong

Yet, having a sight
Ne'er meant seeing right
For with the heart
We blind describe the prickly tip of a dart
And would we remained blind
For in this state sane is the mind

And when dead is the body
The inner man will take it easy
Far from intrigues
And politics
And fly above

The like of a dove
Ignoring the tiny spec of dust
That human's their essence cost
For they amass a wealth of dirt
That nothing brings but pious dearth

Like our mite
Crazy for might;
Our plight disregarding
And man by man slaying
To sooth their madness
By burying humaneness
Our pain must to life bring
Waiting for no bell to ring.

Led by Cain

Remain
Sane
Hug the humane
Treat none with disdain
In earthly struggles that are vain
For wind direction is told by a vane
That can't the havoc stop in its train
Scattering, not gathering, the grain
We need for body and soul's gain
As does our head pouring down the drain
The painful labour of our pain
Wishing in courage we wane,
And flat out like the plain
As he does our brains chain
With us left with no cairn!
Strong and strong we must remain!
Clean, we must clean the stain
By this head, flagged on the pane!

Plume in a Jar

Early in the morning, driving past
Thinking not to see a die cast
With full blown sun on the horizon
Driving thoughts of layers of ozone
Three balloons seen in the air
And a winged flock towards them their way did stir
Divinely soaring
And imperially laughing
And I did gasp: gee!
Who? Me?
Let's see
!
Would someone of the holy,
Holy
Trinity
Tell them
Or tell them
Of the arms checking
And balancing
Each of the three trumps in our deck
Hanging on each others neck!
Freely, the balloons, in the air floated
And freely in the air, at pariahs the birds gloated
Catching a view of them at dead ends scavenging
For earthly salvation scavenging
While a king atop a throne
With a load from afar happily groomed and grown;
Dropping one of their feathers in a jar,
The birds ordered a song for the bar
Behind which king and groomer

Will stand to share the shroud of Mr 'Ceiver
Hurriedly picked
Before on the butt could be kicked
And the plume in a jar dipped
On paper no word skipped.

As I approach my grave

As I approach my grave
Holding firm to my flag of the brave
And seeing all wanting to play save

I, the romantics remember
They would, in their club, have had me member
Not just to swell the number

But to Grace
My place
In the sacred race

Alas! They went
Their wave didn't vent
With the last of them bent

On flagging the metaphysics
With no thoughts of physics,
But the passing time in lyrics

To a container carrying remains
Of what the time harried in his trains
Rather the soul stimulating not just the brains

For this reasoning part dies
While the emotional flies
When the body in the grave lies

To him that approaches his grave
Refusing to be reason's slave

Leaving emotion and fantasy to rave!

The Poet and the Human World

The poet may of the tragic stock be
Never will he of the greedy stock be
He may out of choice a god worship
Never will he cheer the deeds of a warship
Songs calling the downfall of a tyrant he does tune
But dirges to bury the tyrannised his entrails at noon
Spew
For all, not a few!
The flaw of trusting his foible is
The breach of trust from his love, his tragedy is.
A poet is a poet
Human and poet
And a child though
He of mud makes dough,
In pain has one love
In joy has one love
In writing shares either pain and joy
Or both for men with these toy
Espousing the things of this world
Far removed from his world.

To Grace Dethrone

Up there, they always play
We don't as such pray
Here in the house
King there, here mouse
And in the middle
Sounds the fiddle
Invoking Bacchus
Pushing all to bury the curse
But for him in whom euphoria
Dwells in the mind's utopia
And he on this path treaded
And by others discarded
In his flight
Bearing at heart the plight
A pen in hand,
Paper in hand
With the one on the other birthing
In Euphoria pure king
And not excesses
No one sees
Without the subliminal journey
Embarking
And at the politicking barking
Though all the sucker flea
See
None dares point out
For fear of being wiped out
By the king's successes
Feeding his excesses
As they erect

The Courts that correct
Mousy conducts
That miss their docks.

Crown Yourself

For life, crown yourself head of state
And for life drink the dislike of our state
And even in your grave
It shall keep sending the wave
Your spirit is aware of;
Of which we've had enough:
The pot
I Iate hot
Boiling
In poor innocent us
With no nurse
By your slaying
Berated,
Mistreated,
Beheaded,
And Cremated
With your benighted
Hustling you are knighted.

Remember,
Remember
The desert
Your home to be with no lizard,
No! no worm
Bloodily cold or warm
To grace your lightlessness
For only us not ticking time the ruthless
Your breed can trick
Within your wall of brick.

Our laughing spirit in the wood
All bemused when the owls hoot
Thus reject the fruit of your labour
Which you do with your party savour.

Left with the Setting Sun

All in the west stood
None the West understood
All dreamt the West does brighten
So, none to the West refused to listen
Listening to the words'
The commanding words
From the commandments
Transported by regiments
And against stealing
Heavily resounding,
Yet, gimmicking
And politicking
The tyrant mimic
And the masses trick;
And do sublimation introduce
To seduce
And at the state coffers
Beneath our feet, on scoffers
We our eyes cast
And by the storm, off we are cast
Seeing them like our stomachs, empty
And their father of nation happy!

My Good Old Virgin (For Mother Africa)

There she lies in display
Recording time passing everyday
And from time immemorial has so done
And birthed humanity at its dawn
Yet, the Good Old Virgin
Treads on the margin,
The margin of modernity
With her virginity
Far from its highway
And modern man repulses her way
Though with virginity she is rich
Like the modern man with mundaneness his stitch
And my Good Old Virgin I embrace
To prevent herbivores from ruining her grace
According to Wegener a drift
When she wisely engaged to sift
Shedding off the dead leaves
In times of scarcity to avoid thieves
These leaves back and tapping from roots
Human nutrients showing the true roots
Not the force brute by reason brought to bear
On the inner hidden treasure none does wear
Stand firm Raging Good Old Virgin;
Stand as none would ever imagine.

Mother's day 2008, 11/05/08

Yellow Leaf Forever

Old, yellow
With wrinkle
Unseen periwinkle
Yellow
Poor old Africa
Old poor Africa
Looked upon like leaves
Autumn tree leaves
For fall ready to fall
For the world to glory at a ball
You do in you conceal
A treasure seal
With your yellow
The golden gold yellow
In your entrails buried
Where our diggers have us buried.
Thence draws the light of day
Its ray bringing the light of day
To brighten our lost soul
Treated with the dole.

In their golden quest
For your golden chest,
No your Golden Stool,
They did drool
Poor old Africa!
Old poor Africa!
For your unspeakable secret
Their hallow souls did eat
And no wonder they keep

Their arguments cheap
And pit you into endless wars
Hoping you one of their whores
Become, torn and branded leafy leaf.
Yet, you've kept ours forever yellow leaf
Whose brightness our souls brightens
As their dark souls it frightens.
Cheer ye up
Cheer ye up
Your light our wealth
Your darkness their mental health!

Some False God

On knees all praise Jove.
On knees all believe in love.
So of mine I shone a spoke
That made me tremble with stroke
And now in darkness
The star from whom brightness
Was sought, like a lark
Goes mute in the dark
And by it birthed to heap a blame
And would rather good conscience proclaim,
Stroking photophobia
Where assassinated is photophilia
And would of darkness a family make
And dreaming the soul it feeds with cake
Like politicians' promises
Paving their rancid way to high offices
Not the lover's low office to love
And religiously too, painting the world mauve
For the high officer to see
The world discoloured brightly.

Etoudi Royal Rat

The royal rat
In the royal rat
Warren
Does warrant
Our journey out
And would never come out
To face us
But would chant to us
Tunes of royal persecution
And one of royal persuasion
To his lackeys
Forgetting we cats without keys
Will at the gates, patiently wait
Until late
For his Royal Lowness
With astute unholiness
A life prisoner
Himself makes sooner
To keep his tunes alive
And find himself in our hive
We shall dance
We shall dance
Here!
Here! Here!
And go into a trance!
Not in France
Where he would refuge
Seek to avoid the ire of our deluge.

Ghost Lion

Defying the senses known to Hellene,
Stalking the muddy streets of Melen
The muddy Ring Road
The muddy Bamenda-Ekok Road
The muddy Bertoua-Yakadouma Road
The dusty Maroua-Banyo Road
This sleazy
  Shiny
    Flighty
      Filthy
Ghost, a living tyrant
Goliath the giant
Mbivondo
  Of Ewondo
Adorns posts and trees
And in his name weary travellers forfeit fees
And in turn sunken into the ghostly hallow feet
Before the Ghost Lion deprives them of all feed!

Poisonous Heart

The lovely poisonous heart
Beats for no other heart…!
With effusion putting up,
Venom, not blood pumping up
Would scream your best
Interest
Is at heart;
Take your hand and your heart
Would arrest
And send you to rest
And with you resting in peace
In others still would it seek peace`!

K Joiner

Like the storm Katrina sweeps men off their feet
Her act set them quaking in a feat
And they fall for the last first kiss
Ready to cross the ocean for this bliss.

Joiner
Heart rescuer
Stop not to blow
For it will these hearts deal a blow!

Roadside Cross & Wreath

Looking upright
Roadside poles and trees
Avoid upright
Judge who in them sees
Politicians their nose sticking

                                        Here

                    And
There
                    Hiking

          TaxeS
          And
          Rates

                                Now
                    And
Then
E V E R Y W H E R E !
Yet, not all poles and trees flanking
Our roadsides and smiling
And their innocence claiming
Dull up the candle lit cross and wreath singling
Out those that did some hearts freeze
Claiming human lives for fees
And like politicians hiking the toll
And for the living drumming the dole.

The Lawful Theft

Blame the flower for stealing
Stealing all the brightness 'n leaving
In darkness petals
Just as the head opposition's actions stalls
Concealing opposition in a hole
Believing the hole
Does our brains deaden
Shoving any glint down there does brighten
With neither exclamation nor interjection
Driving home to me a question
Why the bright colours of flowers
Intrigue as to why flowers
Easily plug hearts
By humans without hearts
Stabbed
And in gloom the world wrapped
With only flowers left to steal
Broken hearts and pounding hearts still
And why not permit flowers' lawful theft
For only flowers kings' clayey feet cleft.

The Walls of My Love

The concrete walls of my love
Are steel strong gluing my cove
Unflinching to the flame of enmity that burns
But do embrace a fiery passion that turns
Any one hundred and eighty degrees
With or without degrees
To follow their heart
And on their target land like a dart
To their pounding heart still
Cognisant another heart does theirs steal
For barricaded by these love walls
Not even a shelled volley their love stalls
Stalling the freshness of love
Needing neither perfumes nor a trough
'Coz it is oxygen pure
And does a thirst cure
And like the Spring
Does joy bring.

Justice for the Jungle King

All seem in a hubble-bubble!
All do wrestle
And take a test
To show their best
So does the unborn on its way
Stepping out with a cry to stay
Yet, along the way blight strikes
And prayer follows stars and stripes
For the mad lion from the zoo
To jump and hide behind too
And we rather he was in a pit
For he has darkness lit
Darkness we would rather kill
For bringing us wintry chill
Down the spine
And not letting sun shine
With its rays like the mane
Of a lion belly-full in a den;
Mad old lion we won't let you hide
Until you by the laws abide.

The Lion and Attraction

With the Attraction
Of attention
By the beauty of a rose
From its lazing ground, the lion rose
And thought might would
Make him loved in the wood.
Might failed him!
He intimidation embraced to bail him
Forgetting might and intimidation
Words not in Rose's lexicon!

The Last Word

Politicians use words only to deceive.
Poets fashion words to enlighten and convince.

Soon after election forgotten are politicians' words.
Long after poets' death, resonate their words.

For politicians the sword is an armament.
For poets, it flags nothing but an ornament.

For politicians a word is a weapon of mass deception.
And for the poet, it is just a brush for mass decoration

Politicians' mouths like the barrel vomit words to kill
Poets spit words like the dragon spitting fire to still

Driving words to reach the heart like a spear
Or a sword reaching to kill lies politicians tell us here!

Come Shall The End!

Here on earth coffins
Like seraphims
Lined up,
Up, up in the sky up
For their bait
Wait.
The spite of a lion
Our home has made his bastion;
Choosing throne for life
Petering our strife,
Pretending he does not wait.
Yet, for the end coffins wait!
Come shall the end!
Oblivious to his own end;
Ignoring us
And dearth giving us
In dearth, our lustrous cluster
The gloomy glittering spectre
Hail with a welcome
To come
If Salvation, his name is
Though Deliverance we would his name is,
And end this prevailing want
Whose upholder we don't want
Smithing swords
Searing true words
Legating lingo manifold
Devoid of anything largos hold
But something for a funeral song
Day after day sung

To accompany soldiers of poverty
Home to no scarcity!

Our breath we shan't take
Till his dreams we see flake
And like dust blown by the wind
We shall chant in the end we did win
And his funeral sung tune
With freedom to create our rune.

Flirting With the Crown

Flirt and flirt around with the crown
Dreams and dreams 'bound with no crown.
The cool calm and soothing breeze
Veers and brings storm that does freeze
The heat from flirting
       And dreaming
Generated
         'N venerated.
              The chill
With skill
Down the spine
Does the dream refine
To finer dust grains by the wind
Easily blown away from the bin
Where flirting, dreaming and dream
Should dwell and like a stream
Gently flow
        And like passion glow
Where dreams and dreams abound
And there is no flirting ground;
Hand shaking with the crown
Human dreams do drown.

Poet's Heart's Desire

Craving and praying for Peace
He does believe in Peace
Not just individual Peace
But world Peace
And wonders how it can be found
Needing no trumpet to sound
Needing no bark from a hound
To leap on board and homeward bound
Finding Peace streaming from conscience
Needing no science
Calling for lots of Patience
But the interment of nascence.
Gently guiding towards her
He shows she is not far
And that like a star
Far from anything scar
She does shine
With rays so fine
Like the sun's twilight's decline
The Heart's desire's holy shrine.

Not Just Nazi Guilty

The eye empts elf said
The World Bank said
This year growth will be ours
And we danced for hours
Dancing poverty will be slain
Yet, fuel prices brought the strain
And in strength poverty grew
Spoiling us with Nazi coddle to a Jew
And the growth makers stood and looked
Looking at us in the heat to death cooked.

The Grip on our Health

Years now since we had the rain
For years now we've had this pain
When the rain came our way
We sang, rain, rain go away
For we hungered sunshine
Who came and turned us blind
And blind with our minds we see
And would our sight remained at sea
For rain, rain to come again
And not drag our sights down the drain
For we neither love pain
Not strain
And I would all be pain free
And freely fly like the bee
For freedom is that all seek
And not oppression of which I am sick
Grip not our health
Poor rain for it brings no wealth.

Rhythm of the Lands

Otherness, the song others sing
Knowing trouble it will bring,
Steals and kills man's greatest desire
With unrest shooting up in a spire
And in a mire left
With no choice of right or left.
Yet, every Nation has a heart
And even those like ragged mat
Trampled upon with great motion
Need rekindling with oration;
Lying on its ground
Listening to its sound
Beat like a heart!
No, it is really a heart!
That of a Nation for its people
Low, low down to earth needing no steeple
But just one thing: an ear
To do just one thing: listen to hear!
Its music, rhythmical
Its rhythm, musical
Where the steeple with its belfry
Blurs minds like clouds do the sky
On her leaving a rumple
With Nations' heart drumming the trouble.

Song Number 13

I listened to the song and knew it wasn't twist
And pondered and pondered as a linguist
And asked a question
Seeking satisfaction:
Bona, the musician's name was
So, good, I did find it was
And in his first name Richard I found rich
And my dead wish all were rich
Yet, in his drumbeat I found
Good and rich exceeding no bound;
Just song number 13
Not Friday the 13
Elatingly rich spiritually
Latinly elating intellectually.

The tropical singer does sing
Quest not to know what he does sing
For the beats of his drum
The heart of this world pump
And feeling the heart beat
A melody sweet like sugar beet
The dancers enthrals
And the heavy footed appals!

Beat drumbeat, pump the heart,
Turn out warmth like the hearth
And off the stage sweep the bald
Seeking rule with their ribald
And let your beat tell me the plight of man
Drained in loving all he can.

Our Jungle, Their Jingle

The jungle is ours
The jingle is theirs
We of ours paint tableaux
Of theirs, their lies like glass blow
And would our ears with them feed
To lure us away from their misdeed;
Flagging our tableaux shall flag them out
And in droves we shall stick out
And savour joyously the music, verdict
From our tableaux giving their jingle a kick.

Tears for Peace and Love

Passions, humans do express in ways different
Some positions totally indifferent
Some in the aquarium, the gold fish
Freedom deprive and others in their plates relish!

From within my soul I caged a bird
A bird I caged from birth
Making it my everything
When the world turn around to nothing!

Chased out of the window is the dove!
And the tears from my eyes sing for Peace and Love
And query what is to this world left, if the poet
His voice loses and sings not his part in the duet?

Let the tears roll down the cheeks
Let them roll to fill all the creeks
With the poet's natural glove
He wears for mankind to find that grove.

Being all poets let's head for the dove
And bring him home, with our heads up above
Up above the mire of blood they would we drowned
In. Poets do ignominy drag down! Down, down, down!

Dulcet

Like a gentle breeze the music caresses
Human hearts with the softness of fleece
Leaving humans nodding agreeably
Seeing the leaves play the music joyfully
Bringing home the perfumes from lands
Far, far away through which smells to those lands
Transported we are
And thus can see no land is far
For the mind's eye has everything near
And no distant sound away from the ear
And no sweetness of love untasted
Not already tasted
For our everything,
When all is left with nothing
'N by rogues shattered a piece,
Is any dulcet piece.

Travelling on the Spot

Digging and digging they found the rising sun
Through my window I went to the rising sun
On the spot sitting,
Fun loving, fun riding.
The day. Bright and sunny.
And from my brother Sunny
With Aye Ruin
Comes a ring
That spurns such a laugh
That for centuries none ever did have;
Thinking myself a poet
These two point out as would any poet
This rare gem with which we are gifted:
Travelling the world round on the spot seated
With our vocabulary knowing no take off
And never in our journey walking off
And days and days after, I still hear the French
Sweet, smooth and caressing with no cheesy stench:
"Seul homme du monde habilleté
A voyager sans jamais décoler."
And it sparked and still does laugh
                                        Laugh, laugh
As S & his Q-ruin my day brightened
The laughs my days lengthened
And true to my poetic vocation
Never shall I take off for vacation
To feast my eyes on things I freely see
Having no need to voyage across the sea.
Sunny keep shining and brightening
So in our circle we won't break the ring.

The Pair of Blinders

With them on and wallowing in squalid ignorance
And killing time trumpeting the importance,
The importance of things unimportant:
Concepts to be left dormant,
Concepts bi-polarly framed for fame
That has to mankind only left shame
Crimes in the name of communism
Atrocities in the name of capitalism
All done to men in the name of belief
And inexperience quest when for men's relief
If any shall be
And why busy
Caring for capitalism or communism
When there is only one Ism,
The discarded but needed Humanism?
Cage not mankind in those isms
For, there is freedom in my Ism.

Printed in the United States
By Bookmasters